THE LIFE OF A MAN

RON SPICER 1929–1996

COUNTRY BOOKS

Published by:
Country Books
Courtyard Cottage, Little Longstone, Bakewell, Derbyshire DE45 1NN England

ISBN 0 8 98941 06 8

© 1997 Doris Spicer (Text)
© 1997 Dick Richardson (Introduction)
© 1997 Vic Smith (Foreword)
© 1996 Maria Cunningham (For Ron)
© 1996 Colin and Sue Gates (The Last Leaf of the Summer Time)

The rights of Dick Richardson and Doris Spicer as authors of this work have been asserted by them in accordance with the Copyright, Designs and Patents Act, 1993.

All rights reserved. No part of this publication may be reproduced, stored in a retrieval system, or transmitted in any form or by any means, electronic, mechanical, photocopying, recording or otherwise without the prior permission of Country Books.

British Library Cataloguing in Publication Data:
a catalogue record for this book is available from the British Library.

ACKNOWLEDGEMENTS

My grateful thanks must first go to Doris Spicer, widow of Ron. Without her help and encouragement, this book would never have appeared. Most of the photographs here are from the Spicer family collection. I must also record my thanks to The Baroness Trumpington and Vic Smith, who despite their busy schedules, found time to make a contribution in words to the memory of Ron Spicer, and lastly to Maria Cunningham for allowing the reproduction of her song, 'For Ron'.

Profits from the publication of this book are to go to St Catherine's Hospice, Crawley, West Sussex, who cared so admirably for Ron during his last days.

Design & production:
Dick Richardson, Country Books, Little Longstone, Derbyshire DE45 1NN

Printed in England by:
MFP Design & Print, Stretford, Manchester M30 0JT

Origination by:
GA Graphics, Stamford, Lincolnshire PE9 2RB

Government Whip's Office
House of Lords

14th January 1997

I am deeply honoured to have been asked to contribute to this book — what a very good idea to celebrate the life of a real countryman.

My association with Ron occurred during my frequent visits to Old House, West Hoathly. During the 1980s I was the Minister of State at the Ministry of Agriculture, Fisheries and Food. As such I well remember presenting Ron with his Long Service award at the South of England Agricultural Show at Ardingly. Surely noone could have been more deserving.

Ron's pride and joy was the Guernsey herd whose prizes and certificates were testimony to the loving care he gave them.

I well remember sitting in Doris and Ron's house discussing all manner of agricultural matters, not to mention the world's problems at large.

I also remember with huge pleasure the Christmas farm parties at

Old House with Ron playing the piano-accordion, so beautifully, while we all gathered round and sang.

The world is a poorer place without Ron. He and Doris represented everything good in this country. They enjoyed a long and happy life together. Not only did Ron excel at his job but he also gave so much of himself entertaining organisations like the Royal British Legion.

The last time I saw Ron he was very ill, but as always cheerful. I miss him on my visits to Old House — and I shall always remember him with great affection.

Trumpington

The Baroness Trumpington

FOREWORD

This is a book about a special person. Ron was a gentle, reserved individual and his distinctive qualities were not the sort that shouted themselves at you. There was a great deal to the man, so that the longer spent in his company, the more liking and respect was developed for him. Sadly, I only got the chance to see some of these characteristics after he had become terminally ill and had come to accept it. I can say that I have never met anyone who dealt with his mortality in such a profoundly positive way. He had thought long and clearly about the implications for his wife, family and friends and as always, he wanted the best for them.

Doris tells us in this book about Ron's introduction to the wider circle of enthusiasts for the old country songs of Sussex where he made an immediate impact. The initial delight was that the son of such a noted singer was declaring himself as wanting to continue the tradition, but Ron quickly showed us that he was his own man. He was already an accomplished musician but it says quite a lot about Ron that as a 53 year old, he set out to acquire an entirely new set of skills; the ones that involve standing up in front of an audience in concert, festival and club and projecting your voice and delivering and interpreting your songs in a variety of circumstances. At first, he did this with a safety net. Always within earshot was Doris following each line in the book with all the song words typed out, but the need for this quickly died away.

The outstanding memory of these early times was how rapidly Ron developed into a confident performer, able to deal with any situation. If you missed hearing him sing for two or three weeks, you were immediately struck by the progress he had made. Coupled with this was the incredible rate at which he was learning and assimilating new songs from a wide variety of sources. In

Vic Smith, who with his wife, Tina, have a long association with folk music in Sussex. Former co-presenter of Minstrels Gallery on Radio Sussex and co-producer of The Sussex Folk Diary

his mid-fifties, Ron matured as a performer at the rate that one would associate with a developing child prodigy. This meant that his status and popularity quickly grew so that he was having to acquire more skills, like how to cope with microphones in larger venues and in recording and broadcasting studios.

Ron's style as a performer mirrored the wider aspects of his personality. He was a soothing, coaxing singer with an uncomplicated style who seemed to say "Come along and listen to these songs, they are really good!" and, of course, with Ron's interpretation, they always were. George, particularly with songs like *The Barley Mow*, would command attention. His son's style was more engaging and gently persuasive.

He and Doris, always together, became very welcome visitors at all the folk songs venues in and around Sussex and in the last few years this has meant the majority of their evenings. It was a very supportive thing to have Ron and Doris on hand in hundreds of folk club evenings that I compered. Having them there didn't just mean that you had a thoroughly entertaining performer who was adaptable to anything you would ask him to do. It also meant that you had a couple in the audience who paid rapt attention to every performer and radiated enthusiasm for the fine performances of others. They were always positive contributors to that elusive quality of building a good receptive atmosphere that brings out the best in performers.

I have spent many happy times in the Spicers' company but one of the most memorable was also one of the last. I paid a visit not long after it had become clear that he did not have long to live. Ron remarked on the wonderful early autumn weather, said that he would love to see many more of them, but realised that it was not to be. He went on to say that he would have loved to gone on singing until he got into his eighties, just as Bob Copper had, but this was also not to be. These things were said in a reflective, regretful way. He then returned to his normal enthusiastic ways to talk about what he felt was the incredible kindness of the many friends he had made through his music, who were just then inundating him with cards, presents, letters and visits. He told us and Doris that he wanted to see that she would not be neglected after he had gone and that she should still get out to as many song events as she wanted to. Next he talked about his funeral. He had decided the recorded song that he wanted, Bob Lewis was to sing the song that forms the title of this book and then he gave me my part; " I don't want you to be all solemn, Vic. Just talk about me the way you introduce me in the folk club. I don't want people being too sad." So it was with the chapel packed to over-capacity that people found the reserves to give Bob strong but dignified support in the chorus of his song and the ceremony became the celebration of the life of a very fine man. The day ended in the way Ron had wanted with some songs and tunes. Packing our instruments away afterwards, Tina and I remarked to one another that we felt privileged to have taken part.

Vic Smith

FOR RON

Written by Maria Cunningham 26/11/96

This Man of Kent to Sussex came
To do work for a farmer
With ready smile and gentle ways
Our Ron he was a charmer
    He'd play us all a merry tune
    In many public houses
    And bring a smile to every face
    When he sang "These Old Lavender Trousers"

For many years he played his box
At pub and country fair
Then late in life began to sing
His dad's old songs to share
    He'd play us all a merry tune
    In many public houses
    And bring a smile to every face
    When he sang "These Old Lavender Trousers"

From far and wide he gathered songs
To set your heart a-singing
From sad love songs to rousing stuff
That left the rafters ringing
    He'd play us all a merry tune
    In many public houses
    And bring a smile to every face
    When he sang "These Old Lavender Trousers"

Courageously he fought ill-health
And never was downhearted
His smile and music, our great joy
Remembered now we're parted

Ron Spicer 1929–1996

      He'd play us all a merry tune
      In many public houses
      And bring a smile to every face
      When he sang "These Old Lavender Trousers"

Sometimes when you sing a song
Or join in with the chorus
Just spare a thuught for dear old Ron
And all the joy he brought us
      He'd play us all a merry tune
      In many public houses
      And bring a smile to every face
      When he sang "These Old Lavender Trousers"

This song flooded out of me the morning Ron died. I heard the news at about 8am and by 9.30 I had finished the song, or rather it had written itself.

Ron was very special, his love of the music and the songs was infectious and this is how I shall always remember him.

                                          Maria Cunningham

WHAT IS THE LIFE OF A MAN

Harry Holman pictured in the Cherry Tree at Copthorne where George Spicer often sang at song evenings organised by Ken Stubbs. Harry was born in 1888 and after retiring from the railway, worked as a part-time gardener. Known for his singing of What is the Life of a Man.
Bob Lewis sang this at Ron's funeral service at The Surrey and Sussex Crematorium at Worth — a fact I was unaware of beforehand, having already decided on the title of this book!

As I was a-walking one morning at ease,
A-viewing the leaves as they hung from the trees,
They were all in full motion or appearing to be,
And those that were wither'd, they fell from the tree.

Then what is the life of a man, any more than the leaves,
A man has his seasons so why should he grieve;
Even though in this wide world he appears bright and gay,
Like the leaves we shall wither and soon fade away.

Did you not see the leaves but a short time ago?
They were all in full motion appearing to grow,
When the frost came upon them and wither'd them all,
Then the rain came upon them, and down they did fall.

Then what is the life of a man, any more than the leaves,
A man has his seasons so why should he grieve;
Even though in this wide world he appears bright and gay,
Like the leaves we shall wither and soon fade away.

If you go down to yonder churchyard, many names there you'll see,
Who have fallen from this world like the leaves from the trees;
What with age and affliction upon us all,
Like the leaves we shall wither and down we shall fall.

Then what is the life of a man, any more than the leaves,
A man has his seasons so why should he grieve;
Even though in this wide world he appears bright and gay,
Like the leaves we shall wither and soon fade away.

INTRODUCTION

Ron was a *real* countryman, even if he never owned a Barbour, green wellies or a Range Rover, and his picture never appeared in the social pages of *Country Life*. The latter sort, Elsie Maynard from the Queen's Arms at Cowden Pound has her name for – guinea fowl — those who go to town to earn guineas, come home to roost, and are foul (fowl) at weekends! His life reads like the tragic plot from a Thomas Hardy novel. He met Doris when they were children on the farm, fell in love, married and had a family, worked hard all his life and looked forward to a well-earned retirement. He became ill with cancer before retirement and died in St Catherine's Hospice on Tuesday 26th November 1996.

Ron's father, George Spicer photographed outside Cleveland Cottages.

Never wealthy, but always happy; for me Ron and Doris epitomised the old saying 'It's better to be happy with what you have, than unhappy about what you might have.' For Ron was a simple man, not simple in intelligence, but in his demands from life. He worked for Old House Farm for the greater part of his life, and he and Doris could not have wished for kinder employers than the Furse family.

His father, George, was born at Little Chart, near Ashford in Kent in 1906. He was working as a herdsman on a farm in West Langdon, just north of Dover, when Ronald George Spicer was born on 12th January, 1929. They lived and worked on farms near Faversham, Canterbury, Maidstone and Biggin Hill before moving to Sussex in 1940 where George was employed as head herdsman on a farm at Selsfield.

George retired in 1971 but continued as gamekeeper on the farm and lived in Cleveland Cottages until his death in 1981. One of George's great loves was cricket and he served the village for 40 years as umpire. He was also a keen gardener as those who remember the garden at Clevelands will testify. He won over a thousand certificates at village shows for his efforts.

When the Spicer family moved to West Hoathly in 1940, Ron aged 11, met and fell in love with Doris, the seven year old daughter of the carter on the farm.

Ron had begun to play melodeon at the age of five. In those days you only got one day's holiday a year on the farm, and they always went to Margate. They went there with the grandparents and it was Ron's grandmother who bought him the melodeon for 10 shillings. They were living at Faversham at the time, and he never remembered learning to play but by Christmas he was out accompanying the carol singers.

Then they bought him a small 12-bass accordion which he was able to play straight away as he could find his way round the piano. When he was 14 he bought himself a 48-bass instrument and every Saturday night he would go up to Turners Hill and play in the pub there.

There were lots of Canadian soldiers in the area at the time and he made more on a Saturday night than he did in a whole week on the farm. Someone used to take his father's hat off and pass it round the bar, the landlord invariably donating 10 shillings. (Ron's wages at that time was 25 shillings a week.)

Ron left school in 1943 and began working in his boss's garden alongside his grandfather. His grandfather had come to live there in 1940 when the bombing became so bad. He was a melodeon player and would often play tunes with Ron.

During the 1950s George and Ron used to go around in the cattle drovers' lorries and sing and play in the pubs at Turners Hill, Maresfield and around the Ashdown Forest. George did the singing and Ron the playing. Through the singarounds at Elsie's, Dave Toye and Jim Ward met George and often took him to folk

George 'Pop' Maynard who was born in 1872 was also a familiar singer to George and Ron Spicer. Born at Smallfield, he spent most of his life in Copthorne. Known as 'Pop' to distinguish him from his singing cousin, George Maynard of Three Bridges, born c1880.

clubs. Ron remembered going to the launch party of his father's record at The Wheatsheaf, Marsh Green, which was attended by several traditional singers. He often remarked it was surprising he never got involved earlier. The record was called *Blackberry Fold*, a song later sung by Ron.

BLACKBERRY FOLD

As the squire and his sister were sitting in the hall,
And as they were talking to each and to all,
As the squire was singing his sister a song,
Pretty Betsy the milkmaid came tripping along.

'Do you want any milk?' pretty Betsy she said;
'O yes,' said the squire, 'step in pretty maid,
Step in pretty maid 'tis you I adore,
Was there ever a milkmaid so honoured before?'

'O hold your tongue, squire, and let me go free,
And do not make game of my poverty,
There's ladies of honour more fitting for thou,
Than I a poor milkmaid brought up by a cow.'

Then the ring from his finger he instantly drew,
And right in the middle he snapped it in two,
One half he gave to her, as I have been told,
And away they went walking in Blackberry Fold.

With a huddling and struggling pretty Betsy got free,
And with his own weapon she pierced his body,
She pierced his body till the blood it did flow,
Then home to her uncle like lightning she flew.

'O uncle, O uncle!' Pretty Betsy did say,
'I've wounded the squire, I'm afraid he will die;

> All on this fair body he grew very bold,
> And I left him a-bleeding in Blackberry Fold.'
>
> A coach was got ready, the squire brought home,
> A likewise a doctor to heal up his wounds,
> To heal up his wounds as he lay on his bed;
> 'Pray fetch me my Betsy, my charming milkmaid.'
>
> Pretty Betsy was sent for, pretty Betsy she came,
> All trembling and shaking for fear of much blame;
> 'The wounds that you gave me were all my on fault,
> Please don't let my rudeness once enter your thought.'
>
> A parson was sent for this couple to wed,
> And happy we hope is their sweet marriage bed;
> Their sweet marriage bed, my story is told,
> And I left them a-walking in Blackberry Fold.

This song may well have some basis in fact as one of the Featherstonhaugh family of Uppark in West Sussex, did indeed marry a milkmaid in the early 19th century. The song was extremely popular in Sussex and must have given hope to many a weary peasant of 'rising above their station' as they trudged their way home

It is never easy to follow a well known singing father. Ron had a style of his own, drawing songs from both traditional and contemporary sources, always marked with his own stamp. He had a remarkable ear for a good tune and the musical ability to make it his own. Later on he did learn one or two of his Dad's songs, *Blackberry Fold* and *The Cunning Cobbler* among them.

He was always generous with his songs. I remember asking him one evening at Charlwood for the words to *Too Far From She*, and he went to great lengths to make sure I had the tune right. He'd always sing it for me if we were at the same club — sadly the last time I saw him was at The Wellington, Seaford in April 1996.

On the retirement of his father, Ron became head herdsman and remained at Old House until his death. He was always calm and placid and never lost his temper, unlike his father who had somewhat of a reputation for being 'sharp'. He never said a bad word about anyone — and no-one had a bad word to say about Ron.

His father never heard him sing and it was only through the efforts of Jim Ward that he went to the Plough Inn at Three Bridges, Crawley to try 'this singing'.

I was lucky enough to have been there on that night and to arrange for him and Doris to meet the Copper family who had expressed a wish to meet 'George's boy'.

Ron came along with a copy of *The Life of a Man* by Ken Stubbs from which he sung the Folkstone Murder.

The accordion has never really been accepted as a 'folk' instrument in the clubs — until Ron appeared on the scene and charmed and impressed everyone with the way in which he used it. He was always accompanied his wife, Doris, who sat with the words as his 'prompt' and also to rush forward to undo the bottom strap of his accordion.

One of my greatest pleasures of the year was to head for the cattle sheds at the South of England Show to find Ron and Doris washing down the Guernseys for the prize ring. It was on these occasions that he was always in control of the situation.

It was a strange coincidence that three and a half years ago I should move to Little Longstone in Derbyshire where the lord of the manor was Tony Longsdon. For the only time Ron had away from West Hoathly was when he and his father went to work for Tony who then farmed at Cranleigh in Surrey. Tony also had a herd of Guernsey cattle and could be as 'awkward' as George.

Tony told me before he died that they had a few 'uppers and downers!'

The second coincidence was the title of this book. When I heard from Doris that Ron was dying, I suggested that we might write a book together and call it *The Life of a Man* from the old song. Ron had made his own funeral arrangements and imagine my surprise when Bob Lewis stood up and began to sing *The Life of a Man*.

Ron always had a twinkle in his eye, like his father, and inherited his sense of humour as the following two pieces demonstrate.

This is one of Ron's father's that was recorded in the Lewes Arms by Vic Smith, I think:

The school inspector used to come round once a year and look at your work and this particular inspector came to the school and he was walking up and down the rows of desks. He looked at one boy's book and said "That's beautiful handwriting. It's wonderful, what is your name?" He said "John Smith, sir." "Well that is marvellous, marvellous!" So he went down a bit farther to another boy and he saw some more handwriting nearly as good. He said "That is very good handwriting also. What is your name?" He said "Willy Smith, sir." "Any relation to John Smith?" He said "Yes sir, we're brothers." "Wonderful," replied the inspector. So he went down further and he saw a book with blots of ink and writing all over the place. "Dear me," he said. "What is your name?" "Tom Smith, sir." replied the boy. "Tom Smith. You wouldn't be any relation . . ." "Yes sir! They're my brothers." The inspector said "Well how is it. Brothers," He said. "Yes sir, we're triplets." "How is it they're so refined and nice mannered and you're so rough?" "Well, you see sir, when I was born Mother only had two tits so I had to have one of Fathers!" After that, later on, he asked the class whether they could make up a poem. John Smith put up his hand and said, "Yes sir.

There were two little sparrows they built their nest of hay
Along came a storm and washed their nest away."

The inspector said "That is very good, John. Could you make up the second verse, Willy?" He said "Yes sir.

After the storm was over the birds came back again
Plucked up all their courage and built their nest again."

"That's wonderful," remarked the inspector. "Now Tom Smith, could you make up the third verse?" "Yes sir.

There were two little rooks asitting in the shrubbery
They saw them two poor sparrows and tore 'em all to
                                              buggery!"

Ron would sometimes also recite the following and it was no doubt a firm favourite with other cattlemen at the agricultural shows:

I have just given birth to a calf sir
And with motherly pride I am full.
But please do not laugh and pray do not chaff
When I say I have not had a bull
The meadows not nearly the same sir
The farmyard's not nearly so gay
Since the one spot of fun in the cow's dreary run
Has by science been taken away
I have not been loved by a bull sir
I have not had the ghost of a binge
I have not been loved but ruthlessly shoved
With a dirty great brass-bound syringe
Now you may say that's all very well sir
And there's things that us cows shouldn't say
Yet those herdsmen with tarts that play with out parts
Still have it the old-fashioned way.

The Surrey and Sussex Crematorium at Worth, near Crawley, was packed on Friday 29th November when so many people, from all walks of life, came to pay their last respects to Ron's memory. Doris and her two sons, Geoffrey and David, stood for a good hour on that cold, damp evening as people filed past to say goodbye. The service had been more of a celebration of Ron's life, than a solemn ceremony, which he himself had organised. Vic Smith, well known for his long connection with folk music in the county, paid a moving tribute to Ron and Bob Lewis, a fine singer from Sussex, sang *'What's The Life of a Man.'*

Amongst the hundreds of letters and cards of sympathy that Doris and her sons received were these very moving verses written by Colin and Sue Gates of Charlwood:

THE LAST LEAF OF THE SUMMER TIME

Today I heard that you were gone
Away from us too soon
That you had sung your final song
And played your farewell tune.
Today we stand in mournful line
In silence all around
The last leaf of the summer time
Has fallen to the ground.

With that last leaf of summer came
The winter dark and drear
And days would never be the same
With you no longer here.
Now you have withered like the leaves
Of your October song
And silent stand the magic keys
Your fingers danced along.

But the grey of late November
Will brighten into spring
When familiar tunes make us remember
The songs you used to sing.
Today I heard that you were gone
Away from us too soon
And you had sung your final song
And played your farewell tune.

St Catherine's Hospice at Crawley cared for Ron in his last days as they have done for so many others. Proceeds from the sale of this book are to go towards the work that they do. You will find details at the end of this book. If you are able to make a further donation to them, then please do so. The Hospice needs around £2 million per year. They are also in need of volunteers for fund-raising, etc.

Many people knew Ron, though few people who knew him from farming or the dog world knew of his music, and less in the folk clubs knew of his other interests. Certainly we will not forget him and I hope that this book will serve as a tribute to a wonderful man who shall be missed by people in all walks of life.

The last part of the book is transcribed from tape-recorded chats with Ron's widow, Doris, in the days following his death. She knew him better than anyone and the story is best left in her own words.

The estate workers children at Old House c1940. The eleven year-old Ron and his accordion, and on his left is the seven year-old Doris Collins, who was later to become his wife.

RON SPICER 1929–1996

Ron's family came here in 1940. That's the first time they came here, and then they moved away for two years which must have been, I think, about 1945. They left for the simple reason that Ron had left school and worked in the gardens. But then the men came back from the war and of course they had to have their jobs back. Ron's grandparents were living with them and Grandad worked in the gardens as well. And Mr Furse, old Mr Furse stood Grandad and Ron off in preference to a chap that didn't live on the farm and got less money than Ron did. And you know what Dad was like. He said "Well, two of the family have gone and there ain't gonna be a third. I'll give me notice in." So that's what he done.

Ron's mother, Dorothy was from Kent as well.

I met Ron when he moved here in 1940, I suppose, and I was living in the next pair of cottages on the same side of the road. You know where the double bend is — it's all one house now.

I was born at Horncastle, Sharpthorne. My Dad, his father and brother worked for Mr Shelford at Horncastle. He died and they sold the place up, and my Dad moved to the farm here as carter in 1937. I've been here ever since! My maiden name was Collins.

As children we used to go to plays in the drawing room at Stonelands which is opposite the drive to Old House, but it all finished when Mrs Godwin King died.

Ron was still at school when he moved here and he went to Turners Hill. But I went to West Hoathly because I'd just started school, and in those days there were no school dinners or anything, and my aunt and uncle used to live next door to the school, and I used to go in there for my lunch. So when we moved over here, I still carried on.

The estate workers at Old House c1940 taken on the same day as the previous photograph. Ron's father, George Spicer is third from the left on the picture, and Mr Collins, Doris' father, is in the back row between the two women. Note the hats — little seemed to have changed for a hundred years.

Facing page:
West Hoathly. The village where the young Doris Collins went to school. Her aunt and uncle lived in the village. Ron and Doris were married at the church in 1954.

Ron was left-handed and Dad was always going up to the school and telling them not to make him write right-handed. He was always having a row with 'em. Another time his brother Ken came home with a nose-bleed, or something, and Dad said "What you been doing?" And he said "somebody hit me or something". Dad said "Did you hit 'im back?" And Ken said "No! I'd only have got into trouble." So off Dad goes on his bike. They said "Well we don't encourage children to fight back". And Dad said, "No. And I don't want my son to be a wimp either!"

When they were at Cranleigh there was an evening in the village hall — the operatic society done an evening. It was a flop and it finished early and somebody knew that Dad was in the audience and so they shouted out "Is George Spicer in the audience? Come up and give us a song!"

So Dad got up and he sang *Cock a Doodle Doo*.

And the next morning a chap from the village who worked on the farm, came to work in the morning and said "The old vicar ain't half mad with you!" And Dad said "Why? What have I done?" So he said "Well, he thought your song was rude." "Did he?" said Dad. On his bike he gets . . . off he goes.

"I understand you thought my song was rude last night?" "Yes, I did," said the vicar. So he said "Well I got it off a gramophone record, t'ain't the size you're thinking of." He said "Don't speak to me like that. Now I've never been spoken to like that before." And Dad said "We'll you have now!" "You can't speak to me like that," the vicar said. "I'm a canon." So Dad said "It's a pity you don't bloody well go off bang then!"

He didn't get on with schoolteachers and vicars very well!

They went to work for Tony Longsdon at Cranleigh in Surrey and then when he moved back to Derbyshire, they came to work for Beares at Turners Hill.

George and Dorothy Spicer with their two sons. Ken seated and Ron standing behind him. Ron was five years older than his brother.

Facing page:
Turners Hill School which Ron attended as a child, leaving at fourteen years-old to work with his grandfather in the gardens at Old House.
Ron returned in later years to play his accordion for the Maypole dancing and also to sing at a harvest concert.

Ron and his Dad used to race pigeons, and the head gardener that was then, raced pigeons as well. So when they came back to Turners Hill they joined the Ardingly club again. And Mr Brewer, the head gardener at Old House told Dad, "The cows at Old House are in a state and they're dying like ninepins. Why don't you contact Mr Furse as I understand he's sacking the cowman and his son?" And Dad said, "I don't wanna go back to the same job." Mr Brewer said, "Well, you know, I think Mr Furse would want you back. He didn't like it when you left."

So anyhow, Dad did, he applied for the job. And Mr Furse said "I can't understand why you left, Spicer." And he said, "Well you sacked two of the family so I went before you sacked me as well."

Dad said about Ron coming as under-cowman but Mr Furse said "Well the experience I've had of father and son in the two years that you've been gone — I don't really want to do it." But he said "Knowing Ron and you, I'll take you on." So that's what he done.

And then Dad retired in 1971 and Ron took over as cowman. Dad was still living at Cleveland Cottages, Turners Hill, where they first came to.

I can't really remember when Ron stopped racing the pigeons, but Dad packed them up and he carried them on after we were married, and I carried on timing them in for I don't know how long. But Ron could never, because he had to work Saturdays, he could never see them timed in if they came as they were supposed to come and which I always had to do. And then he had a lot of losses with youngsters and getting them trained right up to their first race. And we lost ever such a lot — well the club lost a lot anyhow. Then one day Ron come in and he said "I've had enough. I can't enjoy it, I can't see the fun in it." Because he wasn't here to watch them come home. And he went out there one day and he killed the lot. Just like that. That was the end of that!

RON SPICER 1929–1996

Wakehurst Place, near Ardingly, where the young Ron Spicer worked in the grounds.

Facing page:
*Cranleigh, Surrey.
It was to this village that George and Ron Spicer came to work for Tony Longsdon who also kept a Guernsey herd. Like George, Tony Longsdon could be very 'difficult' — there must have been many battles.*

Ron Spicer 1929–1996

Ron left school when he was fourteen and worked in the gardens for Mr Furse and when he got stood off he went to work in the gardens at Wakehurst Place. Dad was looking for another job and they went to Cranleigh.

Ron and I got married in 1954 at West Hoathly and lived on the farm in a bungalow where the new one is now, for three years when a tractor driver lived in this cottage. The bungalow was ever so damp and the tractor driver moved out. There was only two bedrooms there so we moved here.

Then Dad died and Mum moved up Turners Hill and Ron asked Mr Furse if we could live on the farm, up on the road. But he didn't want us to move up on the road and said if I make an extension, will you stop down here?

When we came here the front room was our living room and dining room and everything — you couldn't get a table and chairs in. If anyone came we had to move the three-piece suite out, so they built the dining and kitchen extension.

When Dad died, Jim Ward said to Ron "Are you gonna carry it on?" And he did, he carried it on ever since. Dad never heard Ron sing — he played the accordion — played the accordion since he was five. I think his grandparents bought him a little melodeon when he was five, just before Christmas. And they went out carol singing, but Ron could never remember learning to play. Then I think they bought him a 12-bass accordion, 'cos Grandad used to play a bit.

They went out carol singing at Christmas. The first night was alright, there was just a few of them, but they collected so much money that all the village turned out the next night and Dad had to turn some of them away!

We used to go out with the cattlemen of a Saturday night to the pubs in area and have a sing song. Ron sometimes played with

Ron Spicer and Doris Collins were married at West Hoathly parish church in 1954.

Dad singing, Dad never heard Ron sing at all. And it wasn't until Jim Ward who run who ran the folk club at the Plough Inn, Three Bridges, and said to Ron "Why don't you come along?" And Ron said "Well I don't know." So he went along a couple of times and people said don't you know any of your Dad's songs and Ron said "No. Not really but I've got Ken Stubbs' book." So they said pick one out and he went back and sang *The Folkstone Murder*. I think we met you there? (They did.)

THE FOLKSTONE MURDER

Kind friends now pay attention and listen to my song,
It is about a murder and it won't detain you long;
'Twas near the town of Folkstone this shocking deed was done;
Maria and sweet Caroline were murdered by Switzerland John.

He came unto their parents' house at nine o'clock one night,
But little did poor Caroline think he owed her any spire;
'Will you walk with me, dear Caroline?' the murderer did say.
And she agreed to accompany him to Shorncliffe Camp next day.

Said the mother to the daughter, "You'd better stay at home;
It is not fit for you to go with that young man alone;
You'd better take your sister to go along with you,
Then I have no objection, dear daughter, you may go.'

Early next morning, before the break of day,
Maria and sweet Caroline from Dover town did stray,
But before they reached Folkstone the villain drew a knife;
Maria and sweet Caroline he robbed them of their lives.

Down on their knees the sisters fell, all in their blooming years;
'For mercy!' cried, "We're innocent,' their eyes were filled with tears,
He plunged the knife into their breasts, their lovely breasts so deep;

The Plough Inn, Three Bridges, Crawley. It was here that Ron was persuaded to sing in public for the first time by Jim Ward. The club at that time was run by Jim Ward and Joan Gifford.

Three generations of Spicers. George, Ron and Geoffrey. Taken outside the former cowsheds at Old House.

He robbed them of their own sweet lives and left them there to sleep.
Three times he kissed their cold pale lips as they lay on the ground,
He took the capes from off their backs, for on him they were found;
He said, 'Farewell sweet Caroline, your blood my hands have stained;
No more on earth shall I see you but in heaven we'll meet again.'

Early next morning their bodies they were found,
At a lonely spot called Steady Hall, a-bleeding on the ground;
And if ever you go unto that spot, these letters you will find,
Cut deep in the grass so green: Maria and Caroline.

When the news it reached their parents' ears, they cried "What shall we do?
Maria has been murdered, and lovely Caroline too,'
They pulled and tore their old grey hair, in sorrow and in shame,
And the tears they rolled in torrents from their poor old aged cheeks.

This murderer has been taken, his companions to deny,
And he is sent to Maidstone jail and is condemned to die;
He said, 'Farewell' to all his friends, 'in this world I am alone,
And have to die for murder far from my native land.

The dismal bell is tolling, the scaffold I must prepare,
I trust in heaven my soul shall rest and meet sweet Caroline there;
Now all young men take warning from this sad fate of mine,
To the memory of Maria Back and lovely Caroline.

Do you remember they had a May Day thing at the Thatch? (Thatched Inn, Keymer.) You said to Ron that the Coppers wanted to meet him and Ron took the accordion down there. We met Sandra (Goddard), and she said "I presume you play? What's your name?" And he said who he was and everyone went mad. And we met Bob Lewis and Gordon Hall, and his Mum was supposed to be there but she couldn't come. George Wagstaff was there, he used to run the Lewes folk club on Saturday. He asked Ron to come down "and we'll give you a floor-spot". It was him that gave him his first booking and it's gone mad ever since.

We went to Sidmouth International Folk Festival twice for the week, and then this year (1996), we just went for the day. Ron also sang at the National at Loughborough.

He done a few of his Dad's songs like *Blackberry Fold*, but he didn't want to be known as George's son, he wanted to be a singer in his own right.

He'd only got to hear a tune once, and if he got the tune in his head, he could pick up the accordion, and it didn't matter what key they wanted it playing in, he could play it in that key. I mean when we used to go to singarounds with the cattlemen or when they used to do things for the old folk at West Hoathly, harvest things, business things or WIs, in Turners Hill. He always played for the Maypole dancing at the school and last year (1995) they had a harvest concert and Ron went up there and sang some songs.

He done just an ordinary singaround — not folk — just ordinary pub songs. Somebody would say to him "Do you know so-and-so?" He would say yes and they would say "Can you play it" And Ron would say "We'll you start to sing and I'll fit in with whatever key you are in." It didn't matter what it was.

He'd never sing a song that he didn't like the tune to. The tune had to come first. Once he got the tune he would write the words down and then he could learn them. When he was at work he used to write the song out on pieces of paper and stick them up in the milking parlour. He'd learn one verse at a time while he was milking or going round the farm. When he'd got that off parrot fashion, he'd learn the next one.

He read music a little bit because he'd had piano lessons, but the trouble was as soon as he got a tune in his head, he could play it! So that was alright all the time it was easy music, but when it got

Ron and Doris Spicer with their son, Geoffrey, and their golden retriever, Flash.

to harder music then he was mucked up. He couldn't read it fast enough. He'd pick the tune up and play it in his own style before he learnt to read the music. He could always read the top line anyhow, the treble; but the bass . . .

I learnt the violin. I got five, er, six certificates from the Royal Sussex School of Music. That's why Ron and I could never play together because I can't play by ear and he couldn't read my music. So we never did play together. I sold the violin and bought our first golden retriever with the money.

We bought our first golden from a person over at Copthorne and they used to show their dogs and they persuaded us to show this. Now I can see the dog wasn't any good really for showing. And then they persuaded us to breed from her and from that we kept one puppy and showed that. That was a better type of show dog. We done quite well with her.

And then we mated her, and her puppy we showed all over the country. We used to go to a couple of shows a week. Anyway if Ron couldn't take me, a friend of ours from Dormansland would. I used to get her ready for shows and they used to take me if Ron couldn't. She was good. In fact we qualified her for Crufts. She went down to Cardiff on the Saturday as a puppy and qualified for Crufts. We then went up to Peterborough the next Thursday and we qualified her mum for Crufts! So we had two at Crufts that year. She went out four years at open shows and she was always in the first three.

But Ron would never show — he would never show the dog. The only time he would ever show the dog was if I'd got a first with Candy and her mum had first prize as well. And then we used to have to go in for best of breed, which was the best golden retriever, and so on. And he used to have to take one of them in then because I couldn't handle both dogs.

The South of England Agricultural Show, June 1988. Ron and Doris, after he had received his 40 year long service award from Baroness Trumpington.

Facing page:
Ron on Salisbury Plain, photographed by Doris in 1968 when they went to see Stonehenge.

He was a judge. He judged golden retrievers. And then of course, with the cattle — I didn't like showing cattle. And then I got older and I couldn't handle them. Only if he got two first prizes, and then I'd *have* to show one. I didn't like it. I'd much rather stay in the stalls and get them ready for the shows, keep them clean, fed and watered.

We only bred the dogs when we wanted a replacement ourselves and we didn't go in for breeding willy-nilly. We tried to mate her and she wouldn't take. We tried three times to get her in pup. She hated puppies and I think that's why she never had any. We sold her sister as a puppy to a couple that lived at Crawley and they became great friends of ours. And she mated her dog to the same one we were going to mate Candy to, and she had a litter so we bought a puppy back. But she was never so good. She done alright in puppy classes. She always carried her tail up high. We mated her and she had to have a caesarean and I said that's it. And we never mated her anymore and we packed up showing.

Ron judged retrievers at Brent and Maidstone. He liked judging. He always said he hadn't got any axe to grind because you know dog showing can be a bit cut-throat. But Ron always said "Oh blow 'em! If there's four classes, I can only give four first prizes. so I'm only going to please four people. So I'll please meself!" He always had good entries and it was always a good show under him. People always knew that Ron was fair.

Ron's one ambition was to get best Guernsey at the Ardingly South of England Show, and he done it. (1991.) He only ever showed cattle in the area about four or five times a year. We showed at the big agricultural show in June at Ardingly, and the autumn fair in October, also at Ardingly. Then we used to go to Cranleigh, Edenbridge and Heathfield.

The first time we went to Heathfield the cattle were all tied up

The Life of a Man

Ron Spicer 1929–1996

Ron, looking very proud standing beside his first car.

Facing page:
Ron photographed beside his motorbike and sidecar with his son, David.

Facing page:
Ron and Doris in the sitting room of their cottage at Old House Farm.

outside, and it tipped it down with rain. We'd got calves there and how they didn't get pneumonia, I don't know. We used to go around and then go in a tent and get a cup of tea, sit down and take our wellingtons off and tip the water out of them! Then start all over again. It got a bit better when they put the sheds up. They all said they'd always had fine weather, but the last year it was outside, it tipped it down with rain.

When we first moved here, there were eleven men on the farm. Then old Mr Furse died and young Mr Furse (the present one), came over from America and modernised the milking parlour. The Guernseys moved from the cowshed to the milking parlour and that's when Dad retired. Ron used to have one weekend in three off. There was three of them — Dad, Ron and Ron's mum's brother. And then Uncle John left the farm, he retired. And they used to have every third weekend off then. One weekend they had Friday off, the next Saturday, and then Sunday.

After John retired and they moved into the parlour, they had every other weekend off. When Dad retired they had the tractor driver and the foreman, who had to work a weekend as well, so then they had two weekends in three off.

Old Mr Furse always called George 'Spicer'. He always said to Ronnie, his son, when George Spicer retires I want Ron to take over, which he did. Mr Ronnie Furse always called him Ron — of course he'd known him since he was a young lad. A year after old Mr Furse died — because they all lived out in America — he took over the farm. Old Mrs Furse was American. The present Mr Furse's children grew up with our two.

Our boys — Geoffrey was born in 1955, David was born in 1959.

There was electricity on the farm here before there was any on the road. My Dad was a carter here and they had five horses and then when he died, old Mrs Furse kept two of them on for a while.

Facing page:
The farm cottage at West Hoathly, where Ron and Doris lived with their two sons, Geoffrey and David.

We got our first car, I suppose it was about 1962, because Ron had a motorbike and sidecar. Neither of us could drive a car because Ron hadn't got a license for one, but he'd got tractor, motorbike and that, but he couldn't drive a car. But he had lessons and he passed first time.

And I said once you get a car I'll learn to drive. And everybody kept saying you'll never learn to drive! You're too nervous, you'll never learn to drive. And anyhow, when we bought the first car I done a hundred mile up and down and round this farm before I ever went out on the road. It was ideal, you could do hillstarts, three point turns, reversing and everything all round here.

I had an instructress from Haywards Heath, she used to own the Bluebell pub at Sharpthorne. We heard that she was good so we phoned her up and she said, yes, she'd take us on. She used to take me out from four till half past five and then she'd bring me home and take Ron out till after seven.

She took me out for the first time, came back and took Ron out. They came back and she said, "Well you can apply for your test and Doris can apply for hers as well." Ron said "Doris can?" and she said "Yes. You sure she's never driven a car before?" Ron said "No."

So he took his test, passed first time, and he used to take me out as well because he knew the test route he'd taken. So we used to go out about every night. When I come to get in her car, I got so used to ours, I made so many mistakes. I couldn't get it into gear or anything else. I was going for my test the next week and she said, "I think you'd better go in your car." I passed first time!

Ron's brother, Ken, is five years younger. He's a bricklayer and plasterer. He had cancer as well, but he's fine now, never been back. Funny how they both had it. Ron's Mum's brother died with it three years ago.

Ron, deep in concentration, holds a rosette between his teeth as he prepares one of the Guernsey cows for the prize ring at the South of England Agricultural Show, Ardingly.

Some friends of ours had a tent. She said "We've got a four birth tent at home, come and make a weekend of it." And Ron agreed to do a weekend first to see if we liked it. I think we went to Cranleigh, the first show. We took the cattle the day before — otherwise we used to get up at four in the morning and take the cattle the same day when it was just a one day show.

So we then went the night before, got the cattle ready, and they used to get home from work and bring the tent over. We thought we liked it and went off for a couple of weekends further afield. Then we went down to the West Country, and then we had a week's holiday. Between us we'd got seven golden retrievers, 'cos we'd got four and Chris and Mike got three. Then we bought a six-berth tent and had that for a number of years. Then we decided that we wanted a bit more comfort so we bought a trailer tent and we used to take that round to shows.

Then we said we'd buy a caravan, which we bought between us, and a couple of months after we got it they came round and told us that they were moving to Bridport. And we couldn't tow the caravan 'cos our car wasn't big enough! It stayed in the garden for a year and then they said they'd sell it 'cos they couldn't take it down to Bridport. So we sold it and we bought our own. It must be about three year ago I suppose.

It was a bit awkward because Ron never knew until Friday night as to whether he could get away. If the hay was ready and that, then he had to help. If it happened to turn wet at the beginning of the week and it was dry at the end of the week. So we always had to wait till Friday lunchtime before we could decide whether we could go or not. So we didn't do a lot until he retired.

Well, in fact, this year was the first year that we did really quite a bit. We used to go away for weekends. We couldn't go away for a whole week, not far, because Ron was having to go to Crawley for

Facing Page:
A smiling Ron leaves the prize ring at the South of England Agricultural Show, Ardingly in 1991 after winning the best of breed — his life's ambition.

chemo every Tuesday. So we only went locally because we belonged to the Camping and Caravan Club. And so we used to go off, and if it wasn't too far and they'd got a holiday meet, we would go down there and into Crawley, have his chemo and go back down there again. Once that was finished we could get away for a whole week.

He was back at work within six weeks of the first cancer operation. Then he started going off his food again, the second time, and we had the bed down here in the sitting room, and he laid down here for fifteen weeks. And they kept saying it's not cancer again. They thought it was lesions from the first operation. He had an ultrasound, an x-ray and a colonostopy and that didn't show up. Then he had an endoscopy and that didn't show up. He had the ultrasound and then you have to wait a fortnight for the surgeon, and then he'd be on holiday so you had to wait another two weeks. Ron was getting thinner and thinner and not eating. And then the surgeon said he would book a barium meal, a full one which tips you upside down. And that's when they found it.

He went in and had another op and was back at work. Then when the foreman, Eric Richardson was 65, he said he wasn't going to work after he was 65 and he'd retire. And Mr Furse said to Ron "What do you want to do?" And by then Ron was 66 and he said "Well with all the trouble I've had, I think I'll retire at the same time." That's how he come to retire.

Mr Furse sold all the cows then, all the milking herd. It didn't upset Ron really. I suppose it did to an extent but after they'd gone he never went up the farm, I mean he worked one day a week after that. Just fencing, or something. Not once did he go round the farm to have a look. He always said I'll go out the gate up the farm and instead of turning left I'll turn right to get the car.

He didn't really miss the cows because of all these restrictions

The Life of a Man

and that. You know all these quotas. As he said, his interest in cows was how much milk they could produce. And of course when the quotas came in and they kept cutting the quotas. You couldn't produce the milk that you wanted to, so they didn't get fed — I mean they weren't starved or anything like that — but they couldn't produce the milk that he wanted to. He lost interest in the milk production side in any case.

Baroness Trumpington is a great friend of the Furse family and she was presenting the Long Service Awards at Ardingly the year Ron got his. And they went to introduce her to Ron and she said, "No need to introduce me to him, I know all about him! We're old friends." She said to Ron once "You're the only person I would miss the racing on television to come and see." She always came to see us when she was here.

I never knew Ron to lose his temper, he was like his Mum for that. Very placid, all the time I knew her, she never lost her temper, and Ron was the same as his mum. He never got uptight about anything really. I can honestly say that in the forty-two years we were married, we'd have arguments, of course we would, but we never had a row. And we done everything together, That's why it's gonna be so hard now. Because it doesn't matter whatever we done, we always done it together. So now I've got to do it on my own.

We hadn't been to the Wellington folk club (Seaford) much this year, because being a Friday night, we used to go off caravanning.

It's very difficult when someone sings one of Ron's songs, but I know I have to cope with it and be stronger the next time it comes around. The first time I went to Turners Hill and somebody sang *Flanders* that Ron sang, and of course, that started me off. This was when he was in hospital and then someone came in during the evening and said "Hello Doris. What have you done with the old

Facing page:
Retirement. From the left of the picture — Mr R Furse, Ron Spicer, Eric Richardson and the late Mrs R Furse.

man?"

I accept that, because it's a new way of life I suppose. I promised Ron I wouldn't give up the clubs and if someone will take me, I will go. The trouble is I don't like night driving. It's the thought of being on my own if I break down somewhere.

Like recently, we came home from Seaford and when we got to the big roundabout, the road going into the tunnel in Lewes was closed. Don't know for what reason but as luck would have it I do know that I can get back into Lewes. But if I'd been somewhere on my own and the road was closed and I didn't know how to get back, I don't know what I'd do. That sort of worries me.

We used to share driving with John Townsend at Scaynes Hill when we went to Lewes. One week we'd drive, and the next we'd leave the car at Scaynes Hill and he'd drive. I can drive to Turners Hill on my own.

George (Wagstaff) likes going to Elsie's and he usually comes here and has his tea, so I can still get to Elsie's. George is working on producing a tape of Ron as he says there is enough material around. Dave Watts told me when he took me over to St Catherine's Hospice to see Ron a couple of times.

Because, Ron was going to make a tape in the middle of November. George had more or less set it up and Piers Bishop, he was going to do the recording and Vic Smith was going to do the notes. John Dudley (who is married to Jill Copper), was going to design the sleeve.

Ron always said if he made a tape he wanted it called *In My Father's Footsteps* or *Following My Dear Old Dad*.

Do you know Maria Cunningham, she's a young girl from Eastbourne. She wrote a lovely thing about Ron and set music to it. She said she sat down and it just came. I said "Are you going to put a tune to it". She said, "I already have!" I said, "When you gonna sing it?" She said, "I was going sing it Thursday Night and I thought no I won't." But I said "Don't leave it too long before you do". I said, "It'll make me cry," and she said, "Well I don't know whether I shall be able to sing it at the moment without crying!"

I doubt I shall go to any of the agricultural shows again. Ron went this year (1996) even though the cows had gone. He got roped in this year to take a Guernsey for another exhibitor into the ring for the championship. They'd won first prize and they collared him to take the cow into the ring.

A few weeks ago — three days the end of September, Ron judged. The South East Guernsey Breeders Association had a judging competition and Ron was judging. He went round to different herds in the area and judged the cattle on the farm. He had three days going round. They picked us up about nine o'clock in the morning and we got back about eight o'clock at night. Thoroughly enjoyed himself. I think we done around five farms a day.

He judged the whole herd. If they wanted, they could nominate just one cow. And so he then judged the one cow on the farm and worked out first, second and third places. And those three days it rained before we went or after we come home — he never put his mac on once. We went out to Tenterden, up to Hawkhurst and down on the coast.

Ron always played his accordion for the May pole dancing at Turners Hill School and then last year (1995) they had a harvest concert. And he ended up playing five songs. And they did country dancing and he played for that.

And we always used to go carol singing round Turners Hill a couple of nights for Turners Hill church and he'd play for that. He didn't do it last year. He didn't feel he could carry his accordion round the village. So he didn't do it last year.

Facing page:
After the award at the South East Guernsey Breeders Association tent at the South of England Show,
From the left of the picture: Ron Spicer, Paul Wyatt, Baroness Trumpington, Mrs Pam Furse, John Brown and Mrs Ida Waters.

I remember we went out one year — actually it tipped it down with rain — there was me with a sort of waterproof thing over the accordion and him playing underneath and I suddenly remembered we didn't have an umbrella. And somebody found a dustbin lid and stuck it over his head! So there was Ron with a dustbin lid on his head, and me holding this waterproof so he didn't get wet.

We were out with Ron singing nearly every night. There was Steyning folk club which was the first Monday in the month — we started going there. This year, actually, we started going. Tuesday night was either Firle or at Elsie's with Jean and Chris Addison. That was the same night as Firle. And Mondays, once a month was John and Di Cullen's down at Tunbridge Wells. Thursday night was Lewes and Friday Night was the Wellington at Seaford. Saturday night was either Turners Hill or Lewes or Elsie's. Sunday night was either The Nelson, Horsham, run by John Byng, or Nellies at Tonbridge, organised by Geoff and Fran Doel. And we used to go to The Rising Sun at Charlwood as well. Colin and Sue Gates were residents here, along with Jim Ward and Iris Bishop. Martyn Wyndham-Read would also get there when he could.

We was out nearly every night. We'd get home sort of twelve o'clock and he used to go round the farm. He always used to go round the farm before he went to bed, and if he thought there was a cow about to calve in the night, he'd sit up until she'd calved. He'd never get to bed before half past twelve at night and always up at five in the morning. He was always the same. It didn't matter whether it was first thing Monday morning or last thing Saturday night he was always just the same, you know. Always singing, learning a song, memorising words.

Ken, his brother, can play the accordion and the piano, but never out in public. When Ron went into Guildford hospital he gave him

Ron Spicer 1929–1996

his old accordion that was about twenty five years old.

Ron's two accordions were too heavy for me to play. One was a Hohner and the other a Scandalli. He only bought it at the beginning of this year. There was a man that lived at Balcombe. Ron used to play at the self-sufficiency show at Ardingly for the Guide Dogs for the Blind. He done it a number of years, he used to take his accordion down and play tunes and he used to get quite a bit of money for them over the two days. And this chap always used to come up to Ron and stand and listen to him and then he'd have a chat, and he came from Balcombe. He said "I've got some accordions, come over one night". Its like everything else, we never did get over there.

And then our next door neighbour said one day that he'd died and his wife wanted to sell the accordions but she didn't know what they was worth or anything. Stuart said he knew that Ron played so he gave him the phone number. So he phoned and said could we go up. So we went over and had a look at them. He'd got three there I think. One wasn't any good at all, the bellows leaked and that. And she'd got this Scandalli which Ron liked and she'd also got — I don't know what the make of it was, but it had 140 bass.

So Ron said, "Well I'll go home". And Ivor Hide from Chard used to do Ron's repairs. So he phoned him up and told him about these two, and what did he think they was worth, and he gave him a price. He said if you can get then at whatever it was. But Ron said he wasn't interested in the other one but he was interested in the Scandalli. He said if you offer a fair price and you can get it at that price, have it.

So he went back and told her, and she said, "Yes I'm quite satisfied with that. My husband would have been proud to think that you were going to play it because I know he liked your playing."

Facing page:
Close to the entrance to Old House stands the White Hart Inn. Renowned in local folklore as the pub where new owners refused to serve George Spicer a pint in his working clothes – a cap and open-necked shirt!
In pre-breathalyser days a landlord could afford to be offensive to customers.

Then he told her how much the other one was worth so that if anyone came round they wouldn't swindle her — he didn't want to make any money out of her. He wanted to give her a fair price.

So we went down to Lewes a couple of weeks later and we were talking to Charlotte Oliver (Spong), and Ron had got the accordion down there. And she said "Oh! Got a new accordion?" And Ron said "It's not a new one, but it's a new one for me," and was telling her about the other one. So she went over and bought the other one!

There was one or two bass notes that I think were a bit squeaky but it wasn't enough to pack it off down to Ivor, so a chap over at Nutley what makes concertinas, Andrew Norman, he done the worst ones. Only Ron would know there was a couple of bass notes that were just a little bit off. Any ordinary person wouldn't notice it. I think Ron took it out about three times — that's all. So that's upstairs now. But that's four pounds heavier than his Hohner. I can't lift it and I can't get the bellows back in once I've pulled them out.

It pleased Ron when he finished his chemo, but he was beginning to go off his food when we went to Sidmouth in August. He was convinced they'd be able to operate again. He finished his chemo and had to wait six weeks and then go and see Doctor Topham for a scan. A week before he was due to go, he had a lump come up on his neck. He hadn't noticed it, and I said "You've got a lump on your neck."

When he went for his six week check-up he told them about it and they took a sample. His legs had started going numb and he told the doctor about it. They said we'll get you a scan done as quick as we can. A week later they told him they couldn't operate again. That really knocked him back. They told him all they could do was try and control it so that he had a reasonable sort of life and shrink the tumour enough to cope with it.

They told him there were three schemes going. One, which is a Hickman line which they can thread in through the chest and you have a little cartridge thing which gives you a certain amount of chemo. They fit a new one every three weeks. But you had to go on computer for that and you were lucky if your name came up, and if it didn't, you weren't. Ken (Ron's brother), had the same thing, and his name didn't come up so he couldn't have it. But Ron's name came up. And so they said that he would be hearing from them during the following week, and he had to go up to the Royal Surrey at Guildford and have this Hickman line put in and then back to St Lukes and have the cartridge fitted, and be shown how to work it and so forth.

He wasn't really keen on it, but he said he'd have it done. Then they rung him up on the Monday and said Doctor Topham wanted to see him on the Wednesday. Ron said "I think I'm going to have my Hickman line fitted." And they said "No. You're not going to have it." That knocked us both back.

So went went up on the Wednesday morning and saw the assistant. She said "No. It's nothing like that but you haven't been off the chemotherapy long enough to have the Hickman line. What we're going to do is take you in today." He said he hadn't brought any clothes up anyhow, he didn't expect it. She said "We'll take you in today and start you on 48 hour chemotherapy and then you'll go home for a fortnight and have that for three months." So Bobby, a friend of ours who'd taken us up, came back and got his clothes and went back up again.

He had the chemo and came home Friday and he was sick and bad. Sunday he was really bad and we had the doctor out. He went back the next fortnight to have the chemo and they deferred it for 24 hours because he was dehydrating.

I 'lost him' that weekend when they told him they couldn't give him any more chemo. The doctor came in, and she said "You don't have to carry on with this chemo you know, Ron." He said "What do you mean?" She said "If it's going to make you so bad, you can stop it."

The boys (Geoffrey and David) aren't interested in the music.

Though after the funeral on the Friday night Geoffrey did sing — he sang *Cock a Doodle Doo*. And Ken sang as well. They was all sitting here singing and I sang *My Lady of Autumn*. Geoffrey had got his Dad's book out there, and I picked hold of it and I said "You can all join in, I'll sing *Lady of Autumn*." And the funny thing is nobody wanted to sing it because they were all frightened they'd upset me. So I sang at it. Everybody knows I sang it. I don't know who's been shouting about — they say I hear you sang last Friday night. And I said "Well Ron wouldn't have been very proud of the way I sung it." Earlier on they said about me singing, and I said "You never have heard me sing and you never will!" And Geoffrey said "If you sing a song, Mum, I will." And I said "Yeh. Like heck I will." And all of a sudden, I don't know why I done it, I just up and got Ron's book — I mean I know the words but I knew I wouldn't remember them that night, got up and sang it and said to Geoffrey "Come on, it's your turn. You said if I sang, you'd sing." So he sung and then blow me if Ken didn't go and sing one of Dad's songs. So all three of us sang Friday night.

But that's what Ron wanted — a good old sing song afterwards. Because when his Mum died, she died in the summertime, about July, I think. After everybody had gone home, there was Ken, his wife and two children, Ron and I and our two boys and our friends from Crawley. And we all sat out there and we opened bottles of home-made wine – 'cos Ron used to make home-made wine, and had a good old sing song and muck around out there.

Ron always said I wouldn't mind having a good old sing song or something like that after I've gone, so I thought, alright, so that's what I done.

Dan Quinn had his melodeon with him, and Will Duke, his concertina, but they had to go early because I didn't realise they were booked that night. Vic and Tina Smith also came with their guitar and concertina.

St Catherine's Hospice cares for people with advanced cancer, Motor Neurone Disease and AIDS and offers them the opportunity to live as fully as possible, whilst supporting those close to them.

We offer the highest possible standard of physical, emotional, spiritual and social care to patients as well as support of their families and friends and carers. Special medical and nursing advice is offered to anyone caring for a terminally ill patient.

St Catherine's achieves this palliative care through the skills of its specially trained staff who provide In-Patient, Home and Day Care, Out-Patient and Lympoedema Clinics, as well as Educational and Bereavement Services.

Our patients are accepted because they need the care we offer. This care is offered without charge and is only possible because of the generosity of our supporters.

It costs over £2 million to maintain our services. We are, therefore, most grateful to you for buying this book, proceeds from which will go towards supporting the work that we do.

St Catherine's Hospice, Malthouse Road, Crawley, West Sussex RH10 6BH
Registered Charity No. 281362